Geology Rocks!

Soil

Rebecca Faulkner

Chicago, Illinois

Editorial: Melanie Waldron and Rachel Howells
Design: Victoria Bevan
and AMR Design Ltd (www.amrdesign.com)
Illustrations: David Woodroffe
Picture Research: Melissa Allison and Mica Brancic
Production: Duncan Gilbert

Originated by Chroma Graphics Pte. Ltd
Printed and bound in China by
South China Printing Company

11 10 09 08 07
10 9 8 7 6 5 4 3 2 1

**Library of Congress Cataloging-in-Publication
Data:**
Faulkner, Rebecca.
  Soil / Rebecca Faulkner.
    p. cm. -- (Geology rocks!)
  Includes bibliographical references and index.
  ISBN-13: 978-1-4109-2753-8 (library binding -
hardcover)
  ISBN-10: 1-4109-2753-9 (library binding -
hardcover)
  ISBN-13: 978-1-4109-2761-3 (pbk.)
  ISBN-10: 1-4109-2761-X (pbk.)
  1. Soils--Juvenile literature. I. Title.
  S591.3.F38 2007
  631.4--dc22
                    2006037062

Acknowledgments
The author and publisher are grateful to the
following for permission to reproduce copyright
material:

Arctic Photo p. **33**; Ardea p. **32** (Bob Gibbons); Corbis
pp. **5, 6, 30, 37, 41 top, 44**, p. **16** (David Aubrey),
p. **13** (Guenter Rossenbach), p. **9** (Joel W. Rogers),
p. **26** (Robert Llewellyn), p.**39** (Sally A. Morgan),
p. **38** (Yann Arthus-Bertrand); FLPA p. **28 left** (Gary
K. Smith), p. **31** (Holt/Primrose Peacock), p. **15**
(Nigel Cattlin); Geo Science Features Picture Library
pp. **5 top inset, 5 middle inset, 7, 8, 17, 18,
20 left, 20 right, 22, 27, 34, 35** (Prof. B. Booth);
Getty Images p. **40** (John and Lisa Merrill), pp. **5
bottom, 42** (Robert Harding World Imagery/Jochen
Schlenker), p. **28 right** (Stone); Masterfile p. **36**
(Dale Wilson), p. **21** (Ledingham/Boden); NHPA
p. **4** (Stephen Dalton); Photolibrary.com
p. **43** (Jon Arnold); Science Photo Library p. **12**
(Bruce M. Herman), p. **14** (David Scharf), p. **25**
(Joyce Photographics), p. **41 bottom** (Michael
Marten), p. **10** (Simon Fraser).

Cover photograph of a seedbed ridged for flood
irrigation, California, USA reproduced with
permission of FLPA (Nigel Cattlin).

Every effort has been made to contact copyright
holders of any material reproduced in this book. Any
omissions will be rectified in subsequent printings if
notice is given to the publisher.

Contents

Any words appearing in the text in bold, **like this,** are explained in the glossary. You can also look out for them in the word bank at the bottom of each page.

THE WONDERS OF SOIL

You probably know that soil is the crumbly material that covers Earth, and that plants can grow in it. Did you know that millions of creatures also live in soil? Did you know that soil forms from rocks?

Soil is very important to us. We need it in order to grow our food. As dead leaves decay, they release **nutrients** into soil. This allows plants to get the nutrients they need to grow from soil. Animals, including humans, get the nutrients they need from plants, or from other animals that have eaten plants.

We need soil for other reasons, too. If there was no soil there would be no cotton plants to make some of the clothes you wear, there would be no trees to produce the paper you use at school, and there would be no wood to make fires and buildings.

Earthworms

In 1 acre (0.5 hectare) of land. There can be more than a million earthworms. The largest earthworm ever found was in South Africa. It measured almost 22 feet (7 meters) from end to end.

⬆ Did you know that earthworms eat soil as they burrow through it? In fact, they can eat their own weight of soil each day.

erosion removal and transportation of weathered rock

Soil forms very slowly. It can take thousands of years for rock to change into soil. Once formed, soil can be washed or blown away by wind and rain, which pick up tiny particles. This is known as **erosion**.

Humans have been growing crops in soil for many thousands of years. In some places this has led to increased soil erosion, because the soil is less protected from wind and rain. Once soil is eroded it produces fewer crops. This is becoming a major problem for food production.

Find out later...

How do volcanoes help soil?

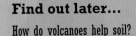

What types of animal live in soil?

How do these trees protect soil?

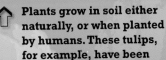
⬆ Plants grow in soil either naturally, or when planted by humans. These tulips, for example, have been planted in rows.

nutrient important mineral needed by a plant for growth

ROCKY SOIL

You can find soil under your feet when you walk through the woods or along a muddy path in the park. It is like a thin skin that covers the body of Earth.

What is soil?

Rocks are underneath the soil that covers Earth. Sometimes the soil "skin" is so thin that you can see the rocks poking through. In other places the soil can be 7 feet (2 meters) deep. In some tropical areas the soil can be about 33 feet (10 meters) deep.

Different types of soil are found in different places. There are over 10,000 different types of soil in the world. You may think that all soil is brown, but it also comes in other colors, such as black, red, yellow, white, and gray. In hot, wet climates soil is bright red and very thick. In cold, dry climates it is gray and thin.

Soil everywhere

Soil covers much of the surface of Earth. You can see it in some places, such as in forests and parks. In other places it is covered by grass or sidewalks, but it is still there.

⇩ Soil is a common feature on the surface of Earth. In some places it is deep, fertile, and full of life. In other places it is thin, rocky, and very little will grow in it.

fertile soil that is good for plant growth because it contains a lot of nutrients

Soil forms when rocks are broken down into tiny pieces, but soil is more than just a pile of broken rocks. The rock particles mix with living and dead plants and tiny animals, as well as water and air, to form soil.

Rocks are made of **minerals**. When rocks are broken down to form soil these minerals are released into the soil. Minerals provide some of the **nutrients** that plants and animals in the soil need to live and grow. When these plants and animals die their remains decay, and the nutrients they contain are returned to the soil. In this way, there is a constant recycling of nutrients in soil.

Useful volcanoes

Did you know that a volcanic eruption can be a good thing? Some of the most **fertile** soil on Earth is formed when volcanoes erupt. The ash that is thrown out of volcanoes contains nutrients, and after it settles on the ground it gradually forms soil.

⬆ Soil around volcanoes is usually very fertile because when the volcano erupts it adds nutrients to the soil.

How does rock become soil?

You may think it is impossible for a lump of solid rock to be turned into soil, but it does happen. Over thousands of years, wind, rain, and ice attack rocks at Earth's surface and break pieces off. This is called **weathering**. Weathering is a gradual process, and it takes place very slowly.

Breaking down rock

There are two main ways in which rocks are broken down to form soil. These are called physical weathering and chemical weathering. Both types of weathering usually attack rocks at the same time.

Parent rocks

The rock from which soil is formed is called the **parent rock**. The speed of weathering depends on the type of parent rock. Harder rocks are more resistant to weathering, but it still takes thousands of years for even soft rocks to become soil.

Frost shattering breaks rocks up to form **scree**. This will eventually turn into soil.

parent rock rock from which soil forms
scree broken rock fragments, usually found on mountain slopes

Rainwater can get into cracks in rocks, and can then freeze. This forces the rock apart because the water expands as it freezes. This is called frost shattering. Sometimes salt crystals grow in the cracks in rocks. Just like ice, the salt forces the rock apart and layers of rock peel off like an onion. This is called onion skin weathering. Both frost shattering and onion skin weathering are types of physical weathering.

Rocks can also be broken down by chemical weathering. When rain falls on rocks the **mineral** grains in the rock may be dissolved by the water, like sugar in a glass of water. This causes the rock to crumble.

Tree roots

When plant roots grow into cracks in rocks they can force them apart and break the rock up. You can see that this happens a lot on pavements, where tree roots have lifted and cracked the sidewalk. If the sidewalk was left for thousands of years it would turn into soil.

The roots of large trees can be so strong that they can break rocks up, helping to form soil.

Mixing the rock

Once the rock has been broken down, the weathered rock particles do not always stay in one place. Some of the pieces of rock may be picked up by wind, water, or ice and transported away in rivers or **glaciers**. This is called **erosion**. When the bits of rock can be transported no further they are dumped in a new place. This is called **deposition**.

All this weathered rock forms a loose layer on the surface of Earth. This is called **regolith**. Tiny plants and animals such as **bacteria** and **fungi** may decide to make the regolith their new home. When these **organisms** die their remains decompose to form **organic matter**.

Forming fast

It takes from 100 to 1,000 years for 0.4 inches (1 centimeter) of soil to form. Soil forms much faster in hot, wet areas than in cold, dry areas. This is because chemical **weathering** happens more quickly when it is hotter and there is plenty of water around.

⬇ When rivers flood their banks the broken rock material they are carrying gets dumped next to the river. Over thousands of years this will turn into soil.

fungi tiny organisms that live in soil

When there is enough organic matter in the newly developing soil, plants will be able to grow. Other animals that feed on the plants will also move in. When these plants and animals die, their remains decay. This adds more organic matter to the soil, so more plants and animals can move in. Any remaining spaces in between the bits of weathered rock will be filled with air or water.

Soil is a mixture of many things. If you fill a bucket with soil from your yard it will contain rock particles, plants and animals (both dead and alive), air, and water.

Chemical weathering

Once soil starts to form the rock underneath it continues to be weathered. This is because the build-up of soil creates the perfect conditions for more weathering to take place. The water in soil can be very acidic, so the rate of chemical weathering can increase, and more soil is produced.

regolith

parent rock

lumps of rock   **plants**   **soil**

parent rock

plants   **soil**

rock

plants

rock   **soil**

Rocks are broken down over thousands of years to form soil.

organic matter rotting remains of plants and animals
organism plant or animal

WHAT CAN WE FIND IN SOIL?

Different minerals

The rock granite contains the minerals quartz, mica, and feldspar. Quartz grains are broken off by physical weathering to produce sand and silt. Mica and feldspar are broken down by chemical weathering to produce clay.

Just as you mix the ingredients together to make a cake, many ingredients are mixed together to make soil. These include:

- rock particles
- air
- water
- organic matter.

Rock particles

Soil develops as the underlying **parent rock** is broken down. The broken pieces of weathered rock are the main ingredient in soil, and form almost half of it. The size of the rock particles varies. There may be pebbles or gravel as well as smaller particles of sand, silt, and clay. The type of parent rock will determine the size and the type of **minerals** that are present in the soil. The rate of **weathering** of the parent rock will determine the depth of the soil.

⬆ The different minerals that granite is made from are broken down over thousands of years to produce soil.

evaporate turn into a gas
pore space between clumps of soil

Air and water

The spaces between clumps of soil are called **pores**. These contain air or water. Both air and water are needed by plants and animals living in the soil. Soil water is also important because it carries **nutrients** from the decaying organic matter that has dissolved into the water.

The amount of water in the soil determines the amount of air that the soil can contain. If the soil is very wet most of the pores will be taken up by water, so there will be little room for air.

Sometimes soil may contain too much water and the excess water forms puddles on the surface. A soil like this is said to be **waterlogged**.

Soil and climate

The amount of water in soil is closely linked with climate. In a wet climate, where there is a lot of rain, there will be a lot of water in the soil. In a hot, dry climate any water in the soil will usually **evaporate**, so there will be very little water in the soil.

waterlogged filled with water. A waterlogged soil has pores full of water

13

Organic matter

Soil is full of life. **Bacteria**, **fungi**, plants, and animals all live in soil, and when they die their remains decay and return **nutrients** to it.

Bacteria

Soil contains billions of tiny bacteria. They have a huge amount of work to do because their job is to recycle nutrients in the soil. They do this by helping to break down (decompose) dead plants and animals. This releases nutrients back into the soil so plants can use them again. For this reason the bacteria are called **decomposers**.

There are a lot of different types of bacteria in soil, with a lot of different shapes. Some are shaped like microscopic grains of rice, and some look like tiny balls. Bacteria live all over soil, and some even live on the roots of plants such as clover.

Microscopic life

Bacteria are so tiny that more than 1,000 of them could fit on a pinhead. One spoonful of soil contains around 6 billion bacteria. This is the same as the human population of the world.

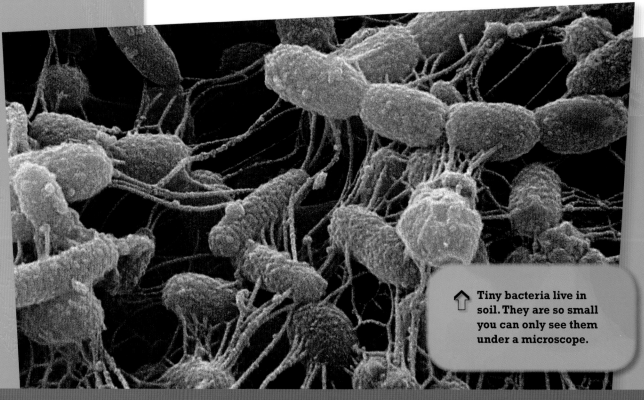

⬆ Tiny bacteria live in soil. They are so small you can only see them under a microscope.

decomposer organism that breaks down dead plants and animals

Fungi

Some types of fungi are also decomposers. They help bacteria to break down dead **organic matter** so that the nutrients are returned to the soil and can be used again.

Other types of fungi grow on plant roots. You may think this would harm the plants, but in fact it does the opposite. The fungi have lots of thin hairs called **hyphae** that spread out through the soil searching for water and nutrients. The fungi therefore help plants to get food and water from soil. These hyphae are so long they stretch over 16 feet (5 meters).

Giant fungus!
The largest living **organism** in the world is a fungus called the honey fungus. In Oregon, a honey fungus was found with hyphae that stretched over a distance of 3 miles (5 kilometers) and covered an area larger than 1,000 football fields Most of the fungus is hidden in soil.

⬇ Many different types of fungi grow in soil. Mushrooms are a type of fungi.

hyphae thin hairs on fungi

15

Plants

Plant roots collect water and **nutrients** from soil in order for plants to grow. Sometimes roots grow through the soil all the way down to the **parent rock**. If they manage to get into cracks in the rock they help to break it up, which creates more soil.

Plant roots also grip the soil to stop plants from falling over. If there are lots of roots in a field, all gripping the soil, they hold the soil together. This is beneficial to the soil because it helps to prevent **erosion**. When the plants die, the nutrients they contain are returned to the soil.

Roots

Plants growing in fields of wheat can have more than 30,000 miles (50,000 kilometers) of roots. These would stretch around the circumference of Earth.

Animals

Lots of animals live in soil. Animals such as earthworms, spiders, centipedes, and termites burrow through soil, mixing it up and creating air spaces. Earthworms eat the soil as they burrow through it. They then leave the chewed up soil as droppings called worm casts. This makes it easier for **fungi** and **bacteria** to get to work on decomposing the **organic matter** in the casts.

← **Plants get the water and nutrients they need from soil through their roots.**

fertilizer substance that is added to soil to improve its fertility

Larger animals, such as badgers and moles, also live in soil. When they dig holes and tunnels it allows rainwater and air to enter the soil. Moles have webbed feet and they cannot see very well. This means they have to sniff out their food, and then use their webbed feet to "swim" through the soil toward it. They churn the soil up as they go. If you ever see a bumpy lawn, it may be because a mole has been tuneling close to the soil surface.

Animals that graze on the grass on top of soil can add nutrients to the soil. Cows leave droppings all over the place, and these can be spread on the soil as a type of natural **fertilizer.**

Avoiding the light

There are more than 2,000 different types of earthworm. They do not have eyes, but they can sense light. They always move away from light because they become paralyzed if they are exposed to it for more than an hour.

This huge pile of soil is a termite mound. Millions of termites live in a nest in the soil below this mound. It is estimated that there are 1,100 pounds (500 kilograms) of termites for every human on Earth.

Humus

The mashed up, rotting remains of dead plants and animals in soil is called **humus**.

When dead leaves fall from trees and pile up on the ground this is called leaf litter. **Bacteria** and **fungi** break down the leaf litter, together with dead roots and grasses, as well as dead soil animals. It then becomes the sticky substance humus.

Humus is dark brown or black, and so it gives most soils a dark brown color. It is decaying **organic matter** so it is a major source of **nutrients**. It also acts like glue, and binds the soil together. This is important because it helps to prevent soil **erosion**.

Helpful humus

Humus acts like a sponge and soaks up water. It therefore helps to keep soil moist, as well as supplying it with nutrients and binding it together. It is very useful stuff.

As **decomposers** get to work on these leaves they will gradually be turned into humus and become part of the soil. In this way the trees are returning nutrients to the soil they took them from.

humus mashed up, decaying remains of dead plants and animals in soil

Humus forms near the top of soil, which is why the soil you see is usually dark. It can be mixed deeper into the soil by burrowing animals such as earthworms. As earthworms burrow down into the soil they take the humus with them. This means the nutrients it contains will be mixed into the deeper soil where plant roots can get at them.

Peat

Peat is a type of soil that contains a lot of humus. For this reason, people sometimes add it to their gardens to help plants grow. In some countries people cut up pieces of peat and burn it to heat their homes.

An average soil sample contains 40 percent rock particles, 25 percent water, 25 percent air, and 10 percent organic matter.

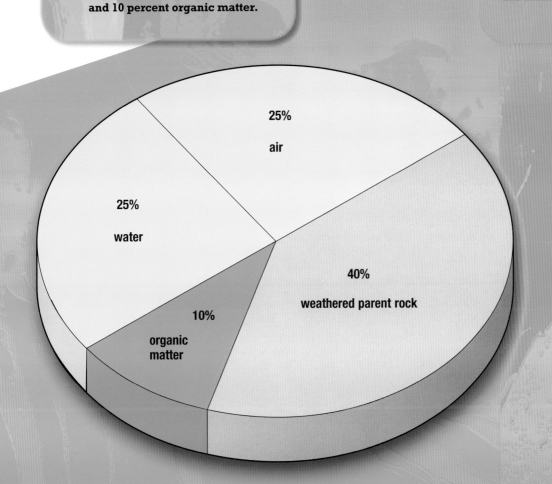

25%
air

25%
water

40%
weathered parent rock

10%
organic matter

What Does Soil Feel Like?

The **texture** of soil is a measure of how rough or smooth it feels. It is determined by the size of the individual particles that make up the soil.

Every soil contains a mixture of different particle sizes. These particles can be sand, silt, or clay. The soil texture is therefore determined by how much sand, silt, and clay it contains. If you take a sample of soil and rub it between your fingers you can feel its texture.

Sandy soil

If a soil contains a lot of sand it will feel gritty. It will also be very loose because the particles do not bind together well. Sand-sized particles are relatively large, so there will be large **pore** spaces between the grains. This means there are lots of air spaces in sandy soils. The large spaces also mean that water, and the **nutrients** it contains, will drain quickly through the soil.

Soil particles

Soil particle	Size
sand	0.005–0.2 in (0.05–2 mm)
silt	0.0002–0.005 in (0.002–0.05 mm)
clay	less than 0.0002 inches (0.002 mm)

These microscope images show sandy soil (left) with large grains and large spaces between the grains, and clay soil (below) with smaller, more tightly packed grains.

aeration number of pore spaces in soil for air to pass through

Silty soil

A soil that contains a lot of silt-sized particles will feel smooth and silky, like soap. It will also hold together better than sandy soil because the spaces between the grains are smaller, so water takes longer to drain through. This kind of soil is often found next to rivers because it forms when rivers dump the **sediment** they are carrying when they flood.

Clay soil

Clay soil feels wet and sticky and can be rolled into shapes. It is made of tiny particles that trap lots of water and make the soil heavy and dense. Particles of clay are so small that you cannot see them without using a microscope. The spaces between the particles are so small that it is very difficult for water to pass through. This means the pores become filled with water, so the soil is poorly drained and is often **waterlogged**.

Lots of spaces

If there are lots of pore spaces in a soil there will be lots of room for air and water to flow freely through it. We say that it is well drained and has good **aeration**.

⬆ Sandy soils are loose and light, and water can flow through them quickly.

WHAT DOES SOIL LOOK LIKE?

Soil particles are clumped together to form lumps called **peds**. The type of ped determines the soil structure. There are four different types of ped:

Crumb

A crumb structure is the best structure for plant growth. The peds are small, about the size of breadcrumbs, so there are lots of air and water spaces. Soils with a crumb structure will therefore be well drained and have good **aeration**, because water can pass easily through the **pore** spaces.

Platy

A platy structure is the worst structure for plant growth. The peds are flat and look like overlapping plates stacked on top of each other. This structure is usually found in clay soils that are poorly drained. There are very few air spaces and plant roots cannot get through.

⇩ If you are lucky enough to have soil with a crumb structure in your yard you should have no problem growing plants.

ped clump of soil

Blocky

In soils with a blocky structure, irregularly shaped and different sized peds are all mixed together. There are lots of air and water spaces, so blocky soils are well drained and well aerated.

Columnar

Columnar soils have peds shaped like columns. There will be some air and water spaces. This type of structure is usually found in deep soil.

Soil structure

Soils can have one or more of these structures, and the structure may change with the depth of the soil. Some soils may not have any structure, they are said to be structureless soils.

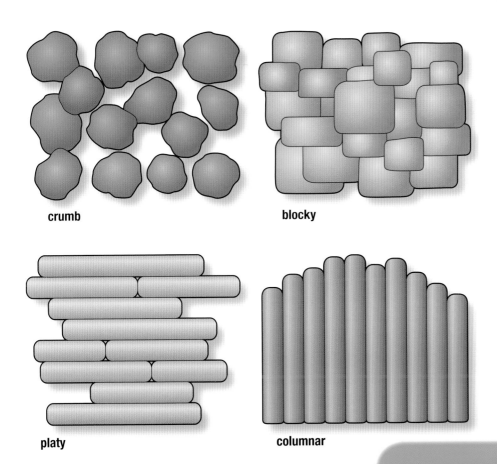

crumb

blocky

platy

columnar

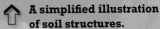

⬆ **A simplified illustration of soil structures.**

Soil layers

If you could cut a slice of the ground, just as you can cut a slice of cake, you would see that soil is made up of different layers. These layers are called **horizons**. The horizons form what is called the **soil profile**.

A horizon

The A horizon is sometimes called topsoil because it is the top layer. It is where plants grow and many soil **organisms** live. **Decomposers,** such as **bacteria** and **fungi,** also live in this layer and break down dead **organic matter** to form **humus.** Rainwater enters the soil in the A horizon and dissolves the **nutrients** from the dead organic matter. The water then drains through this layer, and takes the nutrients with it. This process is called **leaching.**

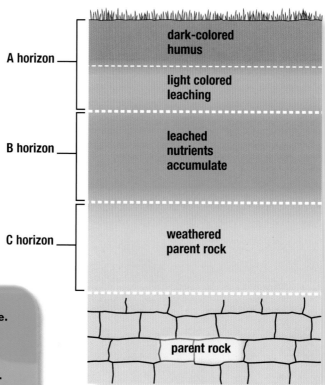

➡ This is a general soil profile. The depth and color of each soil layer will vary depending on the climate and the type of parent rock.

horizon layer in soil
leaching process where water drains through soil, taking the minerals with it

B horizon

The B horizon is sometimes called the accumulation layer because the nutrients leached from the A horizon accumulate here. For this reason, most of a soil's nutrients are found in the B horizon. Plant roots extend into this horizon in their search for food and water. There will be some humus near the top of the B horizon, and rock particles near the bottom. There is very little organic matter in this layer compared to the A horizon.

C horizon

The C horizon can be very deep and consists entirely of weathered rock particles. This layer is too deep for plants and animals to live in, so there is no organic matter here.

Parent rock

Underlying the soil is the **parent rock**. This is the solid rock from which soil forms.

Colored layers

The A horizon tends to be a darker color than the other layers because it contains more humus. The B horizon will be different colors in different soils, depending on the type of nutrients that accumulate there. If the soil is red then it contains a lot of iron. If soil is white it has a lot of calcium in it.

⇦ **You can tell the different layers of soil by their different colors.**

How Can We Study Soil?

A **ped** is a clump of soil. The study of soil is called **pedology**, and soil scientists are called **pedologists**. If you dig up a sample of soil from your yard or school grounds (with permission of course) you, too, can be a pedologist:

- Look at the soil and see if you can identify any **horizons**. What color are they?
- Take some of the soil and rub it between your fingers. What **texture** does it have?
- Look at the shape of the peds. Does your soil have a crumb structure?
- Are there any plants or animals in your soil (dead or alive)? Remember there will be lots of tiny **organisms** that you cannot see.

Remember to wash your hands after handling soil.

Building on soil

Pedologists can also help architects, engineers, and builders. They can advise builders on how deep the foundations need to be for a new building.

You can get an idea of the soil texture by rubbing it with your fingers.

cultivate grow crops in soil

Why do pedologists study soil?

Today, farmers understand that the soil they **cultivate** has taken thousands of years to form. They realize they need to treat it carefully in order to prevent it becoming **infertile**. Pedologists can help farmers use soil in a **sustainable** way, so that it remains **fertile** and is not eroded.

Pedologists can help farmers by finding out what the soil is like in an area in order to determine what crops can be grown there. They can advise farmers what they will need to add to the soil in order to make the soil produce more crops.

Soil maps

Pedologists make maps that show where each type of soil is located. The soils in almost every area of the United States and the United Kingdom, for example, have now been mapped. These maps are used by different people who may be interested in building on the land or using the soil to grow crops.

⬆ A **soil auger** is a long, thin metal tube that can be used to look at a **soil profile**.

Soil all over Earth

There are thousands of different types of soil across the world. It would be impossible to describe all of them in one book. **Pedologists** have therefore grouped soils into different categories. This is called **classification**. There are many different ways of classifying soil, and one of them is based on climate.

Climate, vegetation, and soil

The type of soil that forms in an area will be strongly influenced by the climate. It will affect how much water and air can enter the soil. In a wet climate, the soil **pores** may be filled with water, leaving little room for air. In a dry climate, the soil will contain very little water.

The climate of an area is the type of weather it usually experiences. If an area usually has a lot of rain, for example, we say it has a wet climate.

Climate is one of the major factors that determines where different types of soil form.

classification grouping things together

The climate will determine the type of vegetation that can grow. This will affect the amount of **humus** that can form. The climate will also affect the rate of **weathering** of the **parent rock** because weathering is usually more rapid in hot, wet climates. This will determine how deep a soil is.

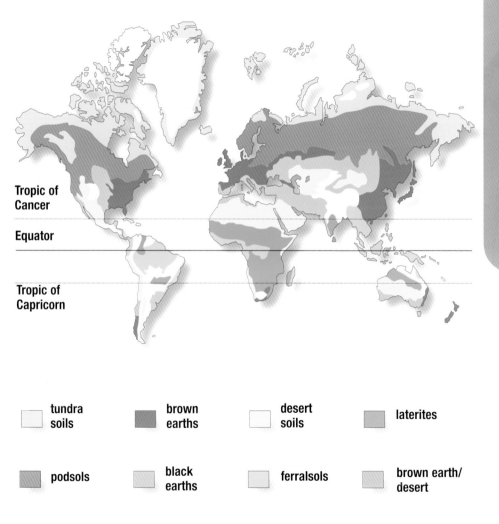

Tropic of
Cancer

Equator

Tropic of
Capricorn

☐ tundra soils

■ brown earths

☐ desert soils

■ laterites

▨ podsols

▨ black earths

☐ ferralsols

▨ brown earth/ desert

☐ other soils

⬆ **The location of world soil types.**

Temperate regions

Temperate regions have two types of soil:

Black earths

In temperate grasslands, such as the steppe in Siberia, the prairies in North America, and the pampas in Argentina, soils called chernozems (black earths) are found. These soils contain the highest amount of **humus** of any soil on Earth.

The grasses that grow in black earths have lots of roots. The humus and roots make the A **horizon** very dark. This soil is ideal for farming because it has lots of **organic matter**, a good crumb structure, and plenty of air and water.

⇩ The types of grasses that grow well in black earths are barley, wheat, and rye. The prairies of North America produce millions of tons of wheat every year.

Brown earths

Brown earths form under temperate forests. The leaf litter is rapidly decomposed to form a large amount of humus, so the A horizon is usually dark brown in color. Brown earths are usually well drained, so may suffer from some **leaching** during heavy rainfall. This makes them lighter in color than black earths. If iron is leached, the lower horizons may be reddish-brown in color. Brown earths are usually around 7 feet (2 meters) deep.

Soil for farming

Brown earths are deep, well drained, and **fertile**, so large areas of deciduous forests that grow in them have been cut down to make way for farming. **Fertilizers** are needed in order to keep the soil fertile.

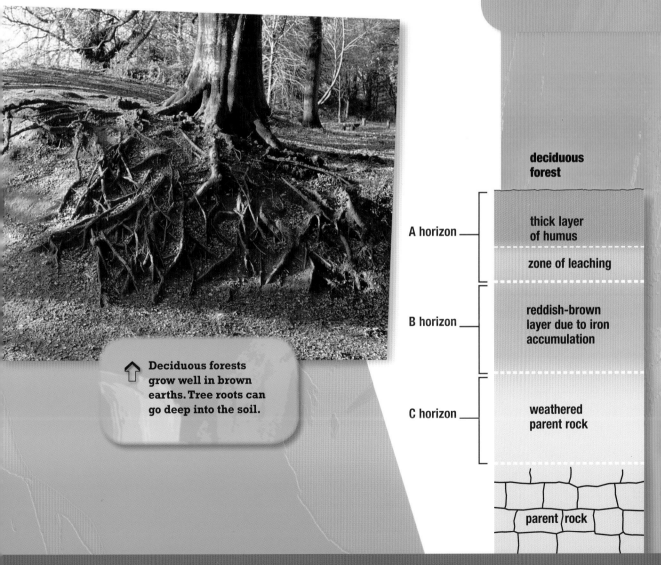

⬆ Deciduous forests grow well in brown earths. Tree roots can go deep into the soil.

deciduous forest

A horizon — thick layer of humus

zone of leaching

B horizon — reddish-brown layer due to iron accumulation

C horizon — weathered parent rock

parent rock

Polar regions

Polar regions have two types of soil:

Podsols

Podsols are found under coniferous forests in northern Russia and northern Canada. These areas experience high rainfall, and there is a lot of **leaching**. The soil has a thin layer of **humus** that decomposes very slowly. This is because the temperatures are low—less than 42° Fahrenheit (6° Celsius) —for more than 6 months of the year.

Water travels down through the A **horizon**, leaching it of all its **nutrients**. This means that the A horizon is often pale in color and looks like ash. The B horizon is often reddish brown because this is where all the nutrients are deposited.

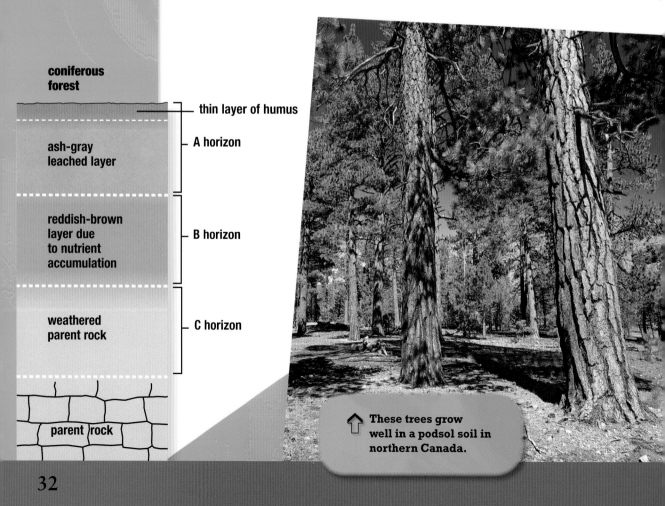

coniferous forest

thin layer of humus

ash-gray leached layer — A horizon

reddish-brown layer due to nutrient accumulation — B horizon

weathered parent rock — C horizon

parent rock

⬆ These trees grow well in a podsol soil in northern Canada.

Tundra soils

In areas with very cold climates, such as further north than the forested areas of Russia and Canada, the soil may be frozen for much of the year. In summer the surface melts, but at a depth of around 20 inches (50 centimeters) the ground will remain frozen. This means water from the melting snow and ice cannot drain through, and so the soil above becomes boggy and **waterlogged**. This type of soil is called tundra soil.

Cold conditions

Tundra soil has a very thin layer of humus because the only plants that can survive the cold are a few mosses and lichens. These decompose very slowly because **bacteria** and **fungi** are not very active in cold temperatures.

⬆ Tundra soil becomes waterlogged in the summer.

Tropical regions

Tropical regions have three types of soil:

Ferralsols

In areas with hot, wet climates, such as the Amazon rain forest in Brazil, the rate of **weathering** is rapid. As a result, very deep soils can form, sometimes up to 100 feet (30 meters) deep. These are called ferralsols and they develop because of intense chemical weathering.

The high rainfall and high temperatures in tropical regions means that plants can grow all year round. Decomposition is rapid because **bacteria** and **fungi** are more active at higher temperatures. All this means that lots of **humus** is produced, but a lot of the **minerals** in it are leached due to the heavy rainfall.

Brick-like soil

Laterite means "brick" in Latin, so it is the name given to this brick-red and very hard soil. It is so hard that sometimes it is cut into blocks and used for building houses. Laterite can also be crushed into the red gravel that you see in tropical fish tanks.

Ferral means "iron," and ferralsols get their name because they contains a lot of iron. The iron makes them a rich red color.

Laterites

Laterite soils form in savanna grasslands, particularly in central Africa, where there are alternating wet and dry seasons. During the dry season the plants die and are decomposed by bacteria in the soil to form a thin, dark layer of humus. In the wet season, **leaching** is very strong, and results in a hard layer forming just below the surface of the soil. This is called laterite. The laterite layer can range in thickness from a few inches to several feet.

Desert soils

In areas with hot, dry climates, such as central Australia, only very thin soils less than 3 feet (1 meter) deep are found. This is because the rate of weathering is very slow, as there is very little water. Not much can grow in the desert, so these soils lack humus. They are often very dry, as any moisture in the soil will be drawn upward and **evaporate** from the surface due to the high temperatures. This means the particles are easily picked up by wind and so desert soils are often heavily eroded.

Amazing plants

Plants that grow in deserts are adapted to surviving without water. Cacti have thick stems that soak up water when it rains. They then store this water and use it during droughts.

⬆ Desert soils can hold very little moisture when it rains, so very little can grow in this soil.

USING SOIL

The main way that we use soil is for farming. Farmers produce crops that provide food for everyone on Earth. Without soil there would be nothing for you to eat, so soil is very important.

The perfect soil for farming?

Sandy soil is good for growing crops because the large **pores** mean that water drains through it. It does not become **waterlogged** and there are plenty of air spaces. However, it lacks **nutrients** because these tend to be leached out of the soil as the water drains through it.

Silty soil is good for growing crops because the spaces between the particles are smaller than in sandy soil and can trap water and nutrients. However, silty soil erodes easily because the wind and rain wash the topsoil into rivers.

Clay soil contains a lot of water and nutrients, but it often becomes waterlogged, so there is no room for air in the soil. If it dries out on a hot summer day, clay soil can become as hard as concrete. This makes it very difficult for plant roots to push through the soil.

Searching for food and water
Some plants are adapted to life in sandy soils. They have long roots that go all the way through the sand into the deeper soil that contains water and nutrients.

If an area has good, loamy soils it will produce a plentiful crop.

delta fan-shaped pile of sediment formed where a river meets the ocean or a lake

The perfect soil for crop growth is one that contains a mixture of sand, silt, and clay. This soil will have a good crumb structure, with large enough spaces for air and water to flow in, and for plant roots to grow. It will also have enough clay to make it stick together and form clumps that keep hold of **minerals**. This soil is called **loam**.

Farmers grow crops, harvest them, and sell them. When the crops grow, they get all the nutrients they need from the soil. Unfortunately, because they are removed from the soil, the crops cannot decay and return their nutrients to the soil. This means that the soil can gradually become **infertile**, drained of its nutrients.

Farmers need to add **fertilizers** to the soil to put the nutrients back. They also need to plow the soil to break it up and improve its structure. If they did not do this the crops would not get enough nutrients, water, or air, so would not grow well.

Delta soil

When a river meets the ocean it dumps all the **sediment** it has been carrying and forms a **delta**. The soil in deltas is very **fertile** because the river sediment contains a lot of nutrients that are continually being replaced. For this reason, river deltas make very good farmland.

⬆ This airplane is spraying crops with liquid fertilizer. Most fertilizers contain nitrogen, phosphorus, and potassium to help plants grow healthy and strong.

How are we destroying soil?

Soil **erosion** is a natural process caused by wind and rain. It is a slow and gradual process that takes place over thousands of years. Soil formation also takes thousands of years. This means there is a very delicate balance between soil formation and erosion, and humans are disturbing this balance.

The rate of erosion is sped up by human activities, such as farming, and in some places soil is now being eroded at a much faster rate than it can form.

Cutting down trees

The main cause of soil erosion is **deforestation**. Cutting down trees to make way for farming and building houses and roads can quickly destroy soil. It speeds up the process of erosion by leaving the soil exposed to wind and rain, and there are no roots under the ground to hold the soil together.

Disappearing soil

Scientists have estimated that around the world, every minute, 50 acres (20 hectares) of tropical forests are destroyed and 49 tons (50 tonnes) of fertile soil are washed or blown off farmland.

The removal of tropical rain forests in Madagascar results in so much soil being washed into rivers that they turn bright red.

deforestation cutting down trees and removing them

When trees are cut down in tropical rain forests the heavy rainfall can wash the soil away very quickly. This means the soil rapidly becomes **infertile**, and so fewer crops can be produced. The result of this is that more forest is cut down to make way for more farmland. In this way, huge areas of the rain forest have been turned into wasteland.

In temperate regions, the removal of hedges to create larger fields for huge farm machinery has also led to increased soil erosion. Removing the hedges means that there is no protection from the wind, so the topsoil is easily blown away.

Valuable forests

The increase in the rate of erosion after cutting down trees is astonishing. In Sri Lanka, where forests have been cleared to make way for farming, soil erosion has increased up to 100 times.

The clearing of tropical rain forests means that there are fewer roots to hold the soil in place, so it is easily eroded.

Bad farming

Bad farming methods can also lead to increased **erosion** rates, so farmers need to be very careful how they use their land.

If too many animals are kept in the same field, they will eat too much grass. This is called **overgrazing**. It results in bare soil being exposed to wind and rain, so that much of it is eroded.

Many farmers grow the same crop each year. This is called **monoculture**. The crops do not die and decompose naturally. Instead, the farmer harvests them. This means that the plant **nutrients** are not returned to the soil and, unless **fertilizers** are added, the soil becomes **infertile**.

⬇ **This land is being turned into desert due to erosion of the top layer of soil, caused by overgrazing.**

desertification process where good farmland turns into desert due to overgrazing

The problem with using fertilizers is that it is very easy to add too much. If too much fertilizer is used any excess may be washed into lakes or rivers when it rains. This fertilizer pollutes the water and causes tiny plants called **algae** to grow. This is called **eutrophication**. When this happens the algae use up all the oxygen in the water, so fish cannot get any and they die.

Farm machinery
When farmers use large, heavy farm machinery for plowing the land it compacts the soil and creates a platy structure. This means there are not enough **pore** spaces in the soil for plant growth.

⇦ Imagine how much the soil will be compacted by machinery this size.

⇨ This pond has been polluted with fertilizers that have been washed off the nearby farmland by rain.

monoculture growing the same crop year after year
overgrazing keeping too many animals in one area of land, so they eat too much of the grass

How can we protect the soil?

If soil is eroded nothing will grow in it. Humans need to try to reduce the amount of soil **erosion**, otherwise we will not be able to grow enough food to feed the world's population.

The good news is that today many farmers understand the need to protect their soil, and so they use many different methods to help reduce soil erosion.

The best way to protect the soil from erosion is to plant more trees where they have been cut down. The leaves will protect the soil from rainfall and the roots will bind it together so it is less likely to be blown away by wind.

Farmers use windbreaks to help prevent soil from blowing away. A windbreak is a row of trees planted between fields of crops to protect the soil from wind erosion.

Traveling soil

Wind erosion can transport soil particles thousands of miles. Soil particles from Africa have been found as far away as Brazil and the United States.

⇨ **Farmers plant windbreaks to protect soil from erosion.**

crop rotation growing different crops each year

When crops are harvested, instead of leaving the field bare and exposed to the wind, the parts of the crops that are not needed can be left as a cover on the field. These help the soil in two ways:

- they protect it from the wind and rain so erosion is reduced
- as they decompose they return **nutrients** to the soil, which reduces the need for **fertilizer**.

Instead of growing the same crop year after year, farmers can grow different crops each year. This is called **crop rotation**, and it helps to keep the soil **fertile** because the same nutrients will not be removed each year. Farmers can also plant "cover crops," such as clover, in some fields each year. These crops cover the soil, and are not harvested so they decompose and return their nutrients to the soil.

In areas of steeply sloping land, erosion can be severe because when it rains the water usually moves the soil downhill. Creating **terraces** or plowing across hills instead of up and down them can help to prevent erosion in these areas.

Terraces

Terraces are like steps in the landscape, and the flat areas can be used for growing crops. They can significantly reduce the amount of soil lost through erosion because the water will soak into the soil, rather than running downhill.

In steep, mountainous areas terracing is a good way to help prevent soil erosion.

CONCLUSION

Earth's land surface is covered in soil. It is home to plants and also many animals, some of which can only be seen under a microscope.

All soil forms very slowly, over thousands of years, as rock undergoes **weathering**. The weathered rock particles are mixed with **organic matter**, water, and air to form soil. As the soil gradually builds up above the **parent rock** it forms **horizons**.

There are many different types of soil throughout the world, ranging from deep-red soils in wet tropical regions, to black soils in temperate grasslands, to thin, gray soils in deserts.

Soil is very important. We need it to grow our food, and farmers have been using soil for thousands of years. Soil is made up of differently sized particles that clump together to form **peds**. The best soil for growing crops is one that has a crumb structure and is well drained with good **aeration**.

Soil **erosion** is a major problem in the world today because in many places soil is being eroded at a much faster rate than it can form. The main causes of erosion are **deforestation** and poor farming methods. It is important that we protect the world's soil because it is a valuable resource.

Loam is the best soil for farming because it has enough clay to keep water and **nutrients** in the soil, enough sand to keep the soil well drained and well aerated, and enough silt to hold the soil together.

FIND OUT MORE

Books

Graham, Ian. *Earth's Precious Resources: Soil*. Chicago: Heinemann Library, 2005.

Gurney, Beth. *Sand and Soil*. New York: Crabtree Publishing Company, 2004.

Harman, Rebecca. *Earth's Processes; Rock Cycles*. Chicago: Heinemann Library, 2006.

Using the Internet

Explore the Internet to find out more about soil. You can use a search engine, such as www.yahooligans.com, and type in keywords such as:
- earthworm
- pedology
- soil profile

Websites

These websites are useful starting places for finding out more about geology and soils:

Smithsonian Soils Exhibit: www.soils.org/smithsonian/

United States Department of Agriculture: www.ars.usda.gov/is/kids/soil/soilintro.htm

Search tips

There are billions of pages on the Internet, so it can be difficult to find exactly what you are looking for. These search tips will help you find websites more quickly:
- Know exactly what you want to find out about first.
- Use two to six keywords in a search, putting the most important words first.
- Be precise. Only use names of people, places, or things.

GLOSSARY

aeration number of pore spaces in soil for air to pass through

algae tiny plants

bacteria tiny organisms that live in soil and break down dead plants and animals

classification grouping things together

crop rotation growing different crops each year

cultivate grow crops in soil

decomposer organism that breaks down dead plants and animals

deforestation cutting down trees and removing them

delta fan-shaped pile of sediment formed where a river meets the ocean or a lake

deposition laying down weathered rock in a new place

desertification process where good farmland turns into desert due to overgrazing

erosion removal and transportation of weathered rock

eutrophication process where too many nutrients end up in rivers, causing algae to grow and fish to die

evaporate turn into a gas

fertile soil that is good for plant growth because it contains a lot of nutrients

fertilizer substance that is added to soil to improve its fertility

fungi tiny organisms that live in soil

glacier slow-moving river of ice

horizon layer in soil

humus mashed up, rotting remains of dead plants and animals in soil

hyphae thin hairs on fungi

infertile soil that is not good for plant growth because it contains few nutrients

leaching process where water drains through soil, taking the minerals with it

loam perfect soil for crop growth

mineral naturally occurring particle. Rocks are made from minerals.

monoculture growing the same crop year after year

nutrient important mineral needed by a plant for growth

organic matter rotting remains of plants and animals

organism plant or animal

overgrazing keeping too many animals in one area of land, so they eat too much of the grass

parent rock rock from which soil forms

ped clump of soil

pedologist scientist who studies soil

pedology study of soil

pore space between clumps of soil

regolith loose layer of weathered rock on the surface of Earth

scree broken rock fragments, usually found on mountain slopes

sediment pieces of weathered rock laid down

soil auger thin metal tube used to obtain soil samples

soil profile arrangement of layers in soil

sustainable activity that means something will last a long time

terrace step in steep land that can be used for growing crops

texture what something feels like

waterlogged filled with water. A waterlogged soil has pores full of water.

weathering breaking down of rock

INDEX